I Can Master
Addition

Carson-Dellosa Publishing, LLC
Greensboro, North Carolina

Credits
Content Editor: Jennifer B. Stith
Copy Editor: Julie B. Killian
Layout and Cover Design: Lori Jackson
Cover Illustration: Nick Greenwood

Visit *carsondellosa.com* for correlations to Common Core State, national, and Canadian provincial standards.

Carson-Dellosa Publishing, LLC
PO Box 35665
Greensboro, NC 27425 USA
carsondellosa.com

ISBN 978-1-60996-953-0

Introduction

I Can Master Addition is the perfect tool for teachers looking for that extra something to help reluctant and struggling students practice basic facts. This book contains standards-based, fun activities including:

- Mazes
- Hidden pictures
- Number searches
- Riddles
- Codes
- And more!

Copy and cut out the "karate belt" bracelets to use as rewards when students master a set of addition facts. Copy and give the award certificate to students who master all of their addition facts within 20.

Table of Contents

Common Core State Standards Supported

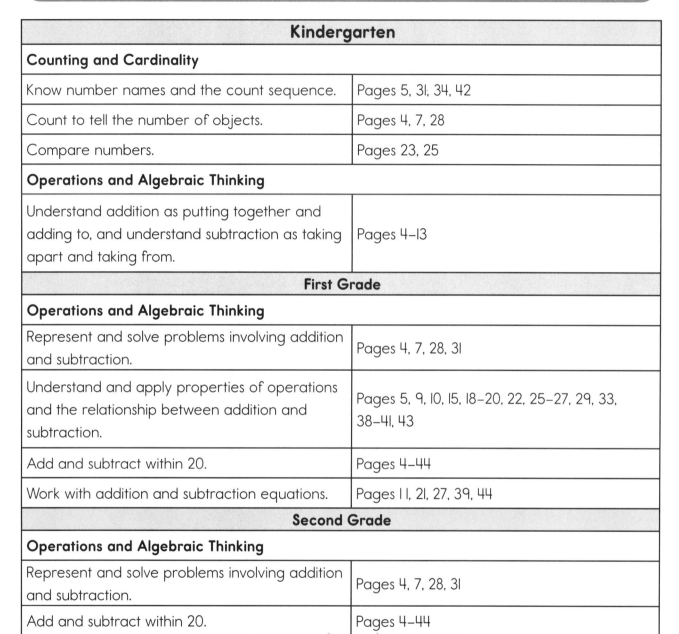

Kindergarten	
Counting and Cardinality	
Know number names and the count sequence.	Pages 5, 31, 34, 42
Count to tell the number of objects.	Pages 4, 7, 28
Compare numbers.	Pages 23, 25
Operations and Algebraic Thinking	
Understand addition as putting together and adding to, and understand subtraction as taking apart and taking from.	Pages 4–13
First Grade	
Operations and Algebraic Thinking	
Represent and solve problems involving addition and subtraction.	Pages 4, 7, 28, 31
Understand and apply properties of operations and the relationship between addition and subtraction.	Pages 5, 9, 10, 15, 18–20, 22, 25–27, 29, 33, 38–41, 43
Add and subtract within 20.	Pages 4–44
Work with addition and subtraction equations.	Pages 11, 21, 27, 39, 44
Second Grade	
Operations and Algebraic Thinking	
Represent and solve problems involving addition and subtraction.	Pages 4, 7, 28, 31
Add and subtract within 20.	Pages 4–44

Tweet, Tweet!

Read the story problem. Cut out the birds. Glue the birds in the correct places.

Ava went for a walk. She saw 4 birds in a tree. She saw 1 bird on the ground. How many birds did Ava see?

Write a number sentence to tell how many birds Ava saw in all.

_____

cut ✂

"Whooo's" There?

Use the color key to color the spaces to find the hidden picture.

Color Key

2 = orange   3 = yellow   4 = green   5 = brown

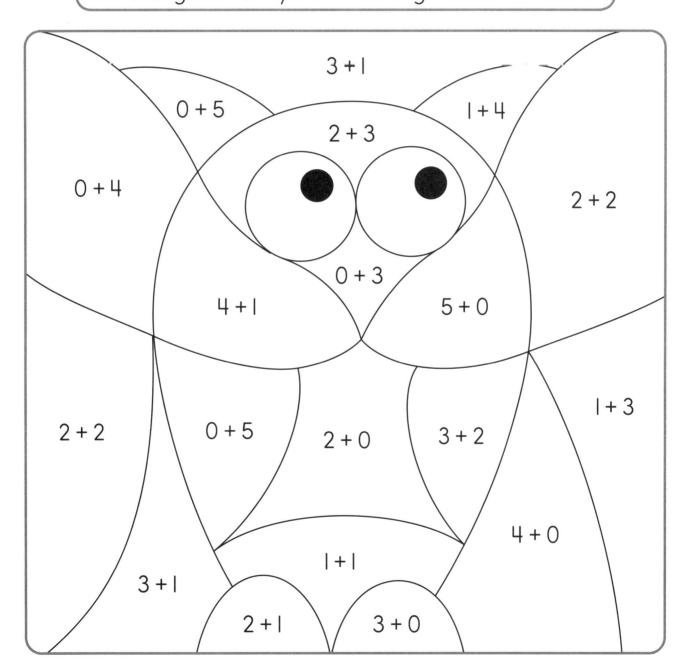

Dive Right In

Write the missing letters to complete each number sentence. Use the word bank to help you.

Word Bank

five	four	one
three	two	zero

1. on____ + t____o = t____ree

2. ____ero + t____ree = ____hree

3. fo____r + ____ne = ____ive

4. t____ree + ____ero = t____ree

5. t____o + ____ne = ____hree

6. ____wo + ____ero = t____o

7. f____ve + ze____o = ____ive

8. thre____ + o____e = f____ur

9. tw____ + th____ee = fi____e

10. ____ne + z____ro = on____

Addition Avenues

Solve each problem. Use the car counters to help you.

1.

2 + 1 =

2.

3 + 1 =

3.

5 + 0 =

4.

2 + 3 =

5.

1 + 3 =

6.

2 + 2 =

7.

0 + 4 =

8.

3 + 2 =

9.

1 + 1 =

 cut

Runaway Robot

Solve each problem. Draw a line through the numbers in the order of your answers to help the scientist find the robot.

1. 0 + 1 =

2. 5 + 0 =

3. 2 + 2 =

4. 4 + 1 =

5. 0 + 2 =

6. 2 + 1 =

7. 3 + 0 =

8. 0 + 0 =

9. 1 + 4 =

10. 2 + 3 =

11. 1 + 1 =

12. 0 + 3 =

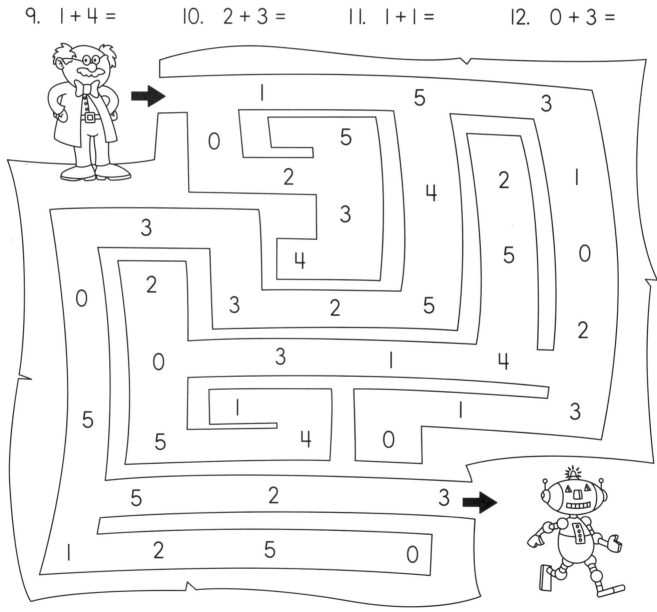

CD-104577 • © Carson-Dellosa

Rainbow Fish

Solve each problem. Use the color key to color the fish.

Color Key

2 = orange   3 = yellow   4 = green   5 = blue

2 + 2 =

3 + 2 =

3 + 1 =

1 + 1 =

1 + 3 =

2 + 3 =

1 + 2 =

2 + 1 =

0 + 2 =

3 + 0 =

4 + 1 =

4 + 0 =

1 + 4 =

0 + 4 =

Fact Flipper

Use the color key to color the spaces to find the hidden picture.

Color Key

4 = gray   5 = blue

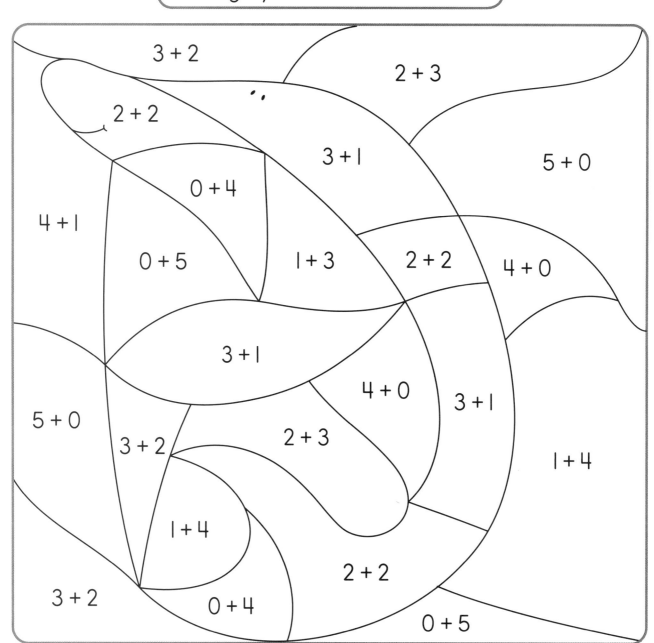

Frosty Facts

Cross out the incorrectly solved problems. (Hint: There are four.) To solve the riddle, write the remaining letters in order on the lines.

1.	0 +2	1	A

1. 0 +2 = 1 **A**

2. 3 +1 = 4 **G**

3. 2 +2 = 5 **R**

4. 2 +1 = 3 **L**

5. 1 +4 = 3 **H**

6. 2 +3 = 5 **O**

7. 1 +1 = 2 **V**

8. 1 +2 = 5 **M**

9. 0 +1 = 1 **E**

10. 4 +1 = 5 **S**

What is the handiest thing to wear when it is cold?

Answer: ____ ____ ____ ____ ____

11

Space Code

Use the key to find each sum.

Key

 = 0   = 1   = 2   = 3   = 4   = 5

1. +  = _____   2. + = _____

3. + = _____   4. 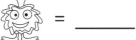 + = _____

5. + = _____   6. + = _____

7. +  = _____   8. + = _____

9. 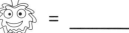 + = _____   10. +  = _____

11. + = _____   12. + = _____

13. + = _____   14. + = _____

15. + = _____   16. + = _____

17. + = _____   18. + = _____

Leafy Lunch

Draw a line through the problems that equal 5 to help the caterpillar eat his lunch.

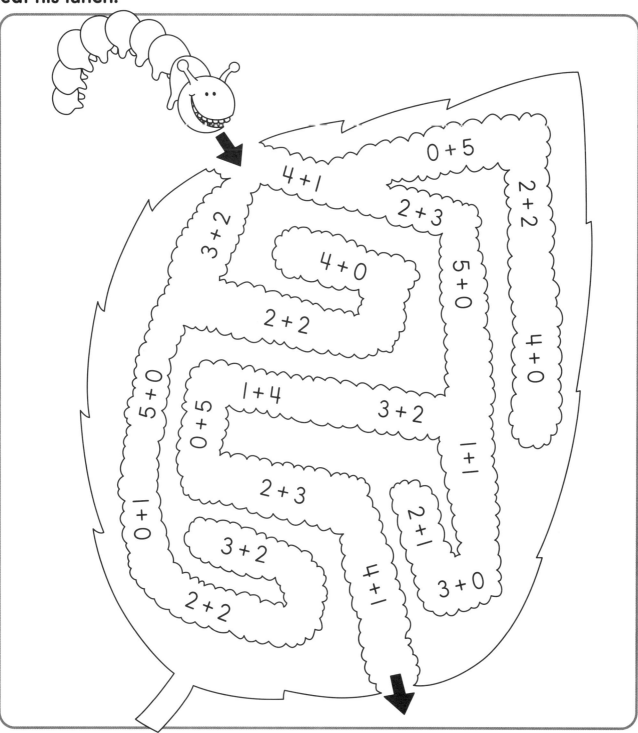

Name_____ Date_____

Buzzing About

Solve each problem. Find and circle each problem and answer in the puzzle. Problems can be found across and down. The first one has been done for you.

1. 5 + 1 = **6**
2. 6 + 2 =
3. 3 + 3 =
4. 4 + 3 =
5. 6 + 1 =
6. 5 + 3 =
7. 6 + 3 =
8. 4 + 2 =
9. 7 + 2 =
10. 5 + 2 =
11. 4 + 4 =
12. 5 + 4 =
13. 0 + 6 =
14. 2 + 5 =
15. 8 + 0 =

CD-104577 • © Carson-Dellosa

Sweet Treat

Solve each problem. Use the color key to color the spaces to find the hidden picture.

Color Key
6 = brown   7 = blue   8 = red

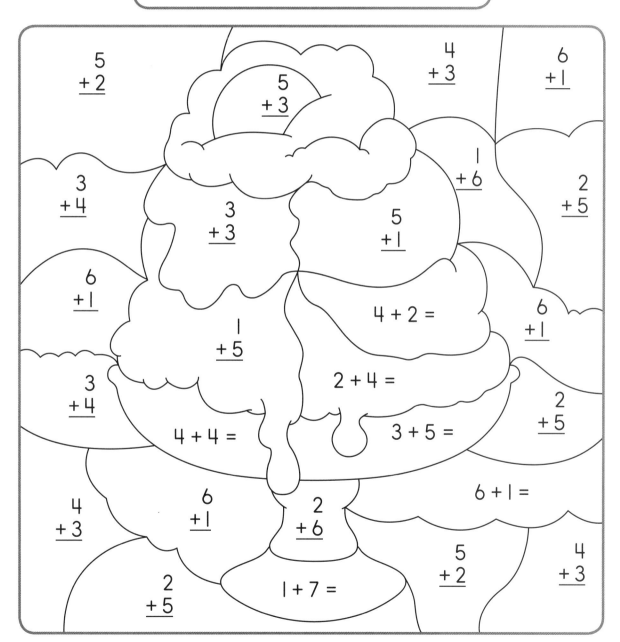

Name_____ Date_____

Flower Flutter

Color the two petals on each flower with numbers that add up to the sum in the center.

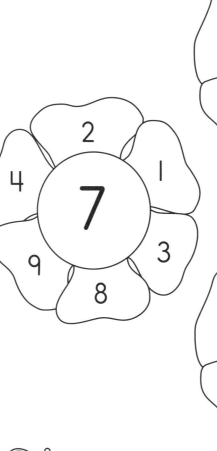

Great Grids

Complete each grid. The first two numbers in each row and column must add up to the last number in the row or the column. The first one has been done for you.

1.

1	0	1
1		2
2	1	3

2.

1		6
8		10

3.

6		6
8		10

4.

	1	9
0		0
	1	

5.

6	0	
7		9

6.

2	4	
5		
		8

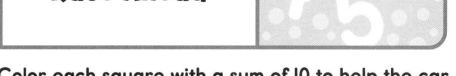

Race Ahead

Solve each problem. Color each square with a sum of 10 to help the car reach the finish.

	5 +5	4 +3	5 +3	2 +6
7 +0	3 +7	9 +1	0 +8	4 +5
5 +1	5 +3	6 +4	9 +0	2 +7
0 +6	7 +3	2 +8	3 +5	7 +2
1 +8	1 +9	6 +2	3 +4	
9 +0	4 +6	8 +2	5 +5	

 CD-104577 • © Carson-Dellosa

Swampy Sums

Cut out the frogs. Glue each frog onto the lily pad with facts that have the same sum as the frog's number.

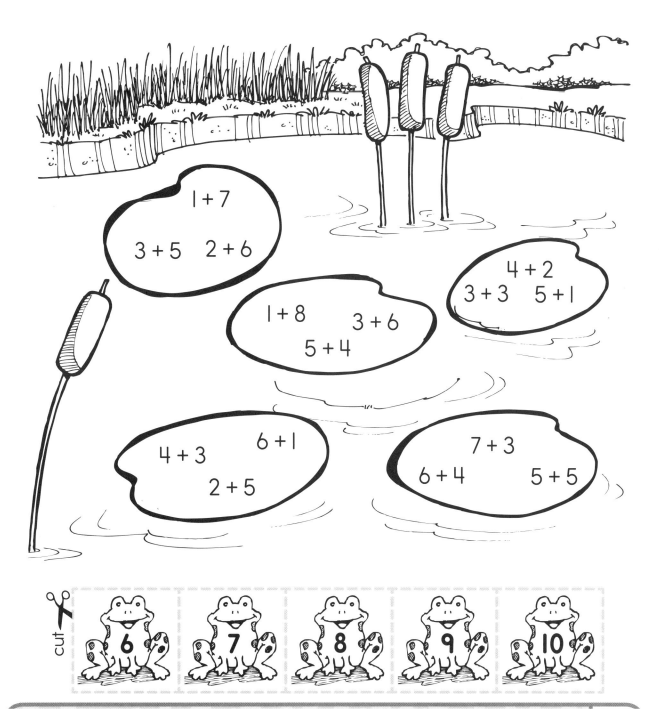

Tic-Tac Math

Draw a line through three facts in each grid that have the same sum.

2 + 4	0 + 2	3 + 2
4 + 1	0 + 6	4 + 4
5 + 2	1 + 1	3 + 3

What is the sum?_____

1 + 6	4 + 4	2 + 3
3 + 3	2 + 6	8 + 2
4 + 3	5 + 3	9 + 0

What is the sum?_____

2 + 8	3 + 1	3 + 6
4 + 2	5 + 4	1 + 6
8 + 1	2 + 2	3 + 4

What is the sum?_____

1 + 4	2 + 2	5 + 3
4 + 3	6 + 1	5 + 2
0 + 5	3 + 6	1 + 5

What is the sum?_____

Tickled Pink

Solve each problem. Use the key to match each sum to the correct letter. To solve the riddle, write the letters in order on the lines.

Key

| 6 = T | 7 = K | 8 = E | 9 = L | 10 = C |

1. $\begin{array}{r} 4 \\ + 2 \\ \hline \end{array}$

2. $\begin{array}{r} 2 \\ + 6 \\ \hline \end{array}$

3. $\begin{array}{r} 3 \\ + 3 \\ \hline \end{array}$

4. $\begin{array}{r} 7 \\ + 3 \\ \hline \end{array}$

5. $\begin{array}{r} 1 \\ + 6 \\ \hline \end{array}$

6. $\begin{array}{r} 5 \\ + 4 \\ \hline \end{array}$

7. $\begin{array}{r} 5 \\ + 3 \\ \hline \end{array}$

Answer: "__ __ N __ I __ __ __ __ S"

Sorting Socks

Cut out the socks. Glue each sock below the correct sum.

7	8	9

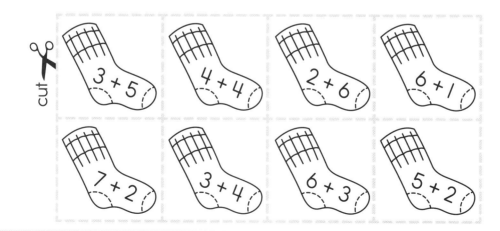

cut

3 + 5   4 + 4   2 + 6   6 + 1

7 + 2   3 + 4   6 + 3   5 + 2

CD-104577 • © Carson-Dellosa

Vroom, Vroom!

Solve each problem. Circle the car whose lane has the greatest sum to show which car wins the race.

1.  5 + 2 =   0 + 9 =   0 + 6 =   4 + 4 =

2. 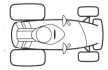 1 + 5 =   3 + 6 =   2 + 8 =   6 + 2 =

3. 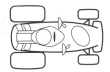 6 + 3 =   5 + 1 =   4 + 4 =   5 + 1 =

4. 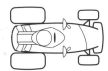 2 + 5 =   7 + 1 =   2 + 7 =   4 + 2 =

5. 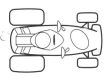 8 + 0 =   3 + 6 =   1 + 6 =   0 + 7 =

6.   1 + 8 =   6 + 2 =   0 + 6 =   3 + 5 =

Finding Facts

Solve each problem. Find and circle each problem and answer in the puzzle. Problems can be found across and down. The first one has been done for you.

1. $2 + 4 =$ **6**
2. $5 + 4 =$
3. $0 + 1 =$
4. $4 + 3 =$
5. $4 + 6 =$
6. $1 + 3 =$
7. $1 + 4 =$
8. $2 + 6 =$
9. $1 + 5 =$
10. $3 + 6 =$
11. $4 + 4 =$
12. $7 + 3 =$
13. $5 + 5 =$
14. $2 + 5 =$
15. $3 + 2 =$

Dino-mite Facts

Color the number of dinosaurs for the first number in each fact yellow.
Color the number of dinosaurs for the second number in each fact
green.

8 + 0

7 + 1

6 + 2

5 + 3

4 + 4

3 + 5

2 + 6

0 + 8

What is the sum of each fact? _____

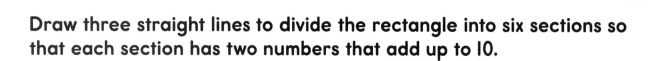

Dividing Lines

Draw three straight lines to divide the rectangle into six sections so that each section has two numbers that add up to 10.

7

0

6

3

10

5

4

1

2

5   9

8

Fishing for Answers

Circle the number sentences that are correct in each group. To solve the riddle, write the remaining letters in order on the lines.

1. $3 + 7 = 10$ **N**
    $6 + 4 = 10$ **S**
    $8 + 3 = 10$ **A**
    $9 + 1 = 10$ **L**

2. $2 + 2 = 4$ **C**
    $5 + 1 = 4$ **G**
    $1 + 3 = 4$ **E**
    $3 + 1 - 4$ **D**

3. $5 + 0 = 5$ **U**
    $4 + 2 = 5$ **O**
    $1 + 4 = 5$ **A**
    $4 + 1 = 5$ **I**

4. $5 + 1 = 6$ **M**
    $2 + 3 = 6$ **L**
    $2 + 4 = 6$ **N**
    $3 + 3 = 6$ **R**

5. $1 + 6 = 7$ **F**
    $6 + 4 = 7$ **D**
    $6 + 1 = 7$ **E**
    $5 + 2 = 7$ **G**

6. $5 + 2 = 3$ **F**
    $0 + 3 = 3$ **J**
    $2 + 1 = 3$ **L**
    $3 + 0 = 3$ **K**

7. $5 + 5 = 10$ **O**
    $7 + 3 = 10$ **L**
    $4 + 6 = 10$ **J**
    $8 + 1 = 10$ **I**

8. $1 + 8 = 9$ **R**
    $7 + 2 = 9$ **T**
    $6 + 2 = 9$ **S**
    $5 + 4 = 9$ **N**

9. $3 + 5 = 8$ **R**
    $8 + 5 = 8$ **H**
    $4 + 4 = 8$ **S**
    $2 + 6 = 8$ **T**

What is the most expensive fish?

Answer: ___ ___ ___ ___ ___ ___ ___ ___ ___

Fruit Baskets

Solve each problem. Use the apple counters to help you.

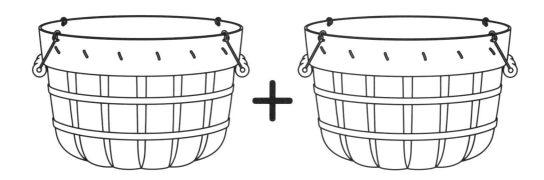

1. 6 + 4 = _____

2. 5 + 1 = _____

3. 6 + 3 = _____

4. 3 + 4 = _____

5. 7 + 2 = _____

6. 3 + 7 = _____

7. 5 + 5 = _____

8. 6 + 3 = _____

9. 9 + 1 = _____

10. 4 + 5 = _____

11. 8 + 2 = _____

12. 9 + 0 = _____

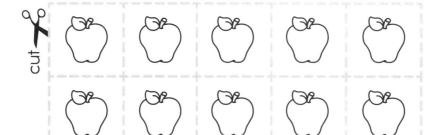

cut

Finding Fifteen

Find and color the 15 pairs of squares with numbers that add up to 15. Pairs can be found across and down. The first pair has been done for you.

7	9	14	1	3	0	4
8	2	9	8	7	13	11
0	3	13	2	9	6	1
15	8	4	8	7	5	3
11	3	10	1	15	1	4
4	12	5	14	4	8	11
2	9	6	8	3	15	0

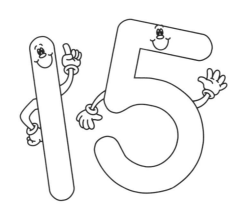

Doghouse Addition

Solve each problem. Find and circle each problem and answer in the puzzle. Problems can be found across and down. The first one has been done for you.

1. $6 + 9 = \mathbf{15}$ 2. $8 + 3 =$ 3. $7 + 8 =$

4. $5 + 8 =$ 5. $4 + 8 =$ 6. $4 + 9 =$

7. $9 + 3 =$ 8. $2 + 9 =$ 9. $5 + 9 =$

10. $6 + 8 =$ 11. $9 + 2 =$ 12. $7 + 7 =$

13. $6 + 6 =$ 14. $10 + 3 =$ 15. $9 + 6 =$

Domino Facts

Solve each problem. Write the sum.

1. 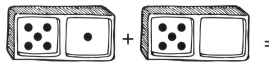 =

_____

2. 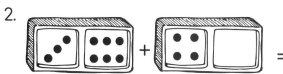 =

_____

3. + =

_____

4. 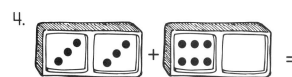 =

_____

5. + =

_____

6. 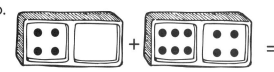 =

_____

7. + =

_____

8.  =

_____

The Cat's Meow

Solve each problem. Circle the correct sum and its letter. To solve the riddle, write the circled letters in order on the lines. The first one has been done for you.

1. 1 + 9 =

 ⑩ 11 12

 Ⓣ F E

2. 4 + 8 =

 10 11 12

 D J H

3. 7 + 3 =

 10 11 12

 R S T

4. 9 + 2 =

 10 11 12

 D E F

5. 5 + 7 =

 10 11 12

 O A E

6. 8 + 3 =

 10 11 12

 A B C

7. 9 + 3 =

 10 11 12

 K M L

8. 4 + 6 =

 10 11 12

 I J K

9. 6 + 5 =

 10 11 12

 M N O

10. 7 + 4 =

 10 11 12

 C D E

11. 6 + 6 =

 10 11 12

 O N M

12. 10 + 1 =

 10 11 12

 G I H

13. 11 + 1 =

 10 11 12

 D E C

14. 10 + 2 =

 10 11 12

 O A E

What song does a cat like best?

Answer: " _T_ ____ ____ ____ ____

____ ____ ____ ____ ____ ____ "

Slices of Pizza

Draw two straight lines to divide each pizza into four slices so that each slice has two numbers that add up to the sum shown.

11

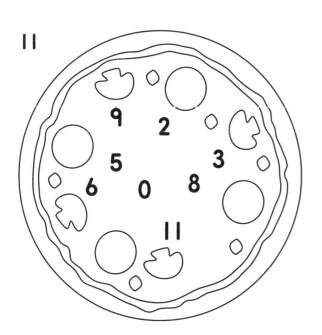

12

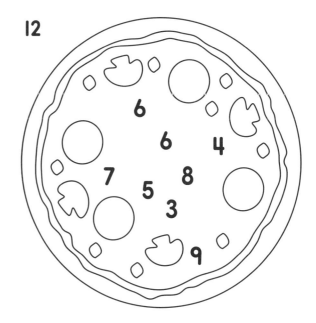

13

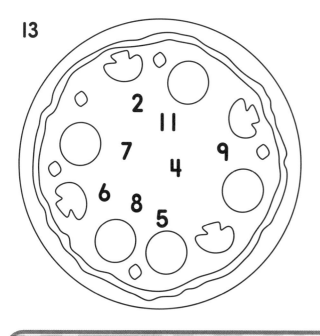

14

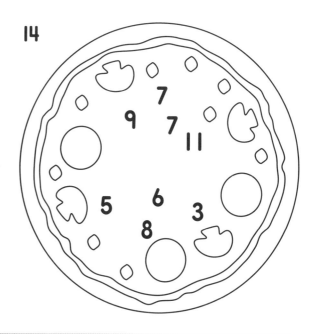

A Sweet Puzzle

Solve each problem. Write the number word for each answer in the puzzle.

Across
1. 3 + 14 =
5. 10 + 10 =
6. 10 + 9 =

Down
2. 6 + 12 =
3. 19 + 1 =
4. 11 + 8 =

Name_____ Date_____

Pond Problems

Draw a line through the problems that equal 18 to help the duck find the pond.

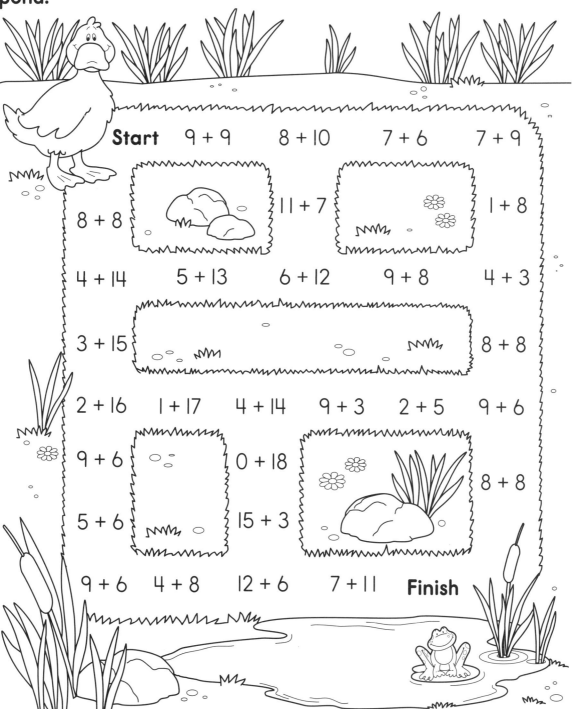

Start   9 + 9   8 + 10   7 + 6   7 + 9

8 + 8   11 + 7   1 + 8

4 + 14   5 + 13   6 + 12   9 + 8   4 + 3

3 + 15   8 + 8

2 + 16   1 + 17   4 + 14   9 + 3   2 + 5   9 + 6

9 + 6   0 + 18   8 + 8

5 + 6   15 + 3

9 + 6   4 + 8   12 + 6   7 + 11   **Finish**

Name_____   Date_____

Blending In

Use the color key to color the spaces to find the hidden picture.

Color Key

16 = orange   17 = yellow   18 = blue

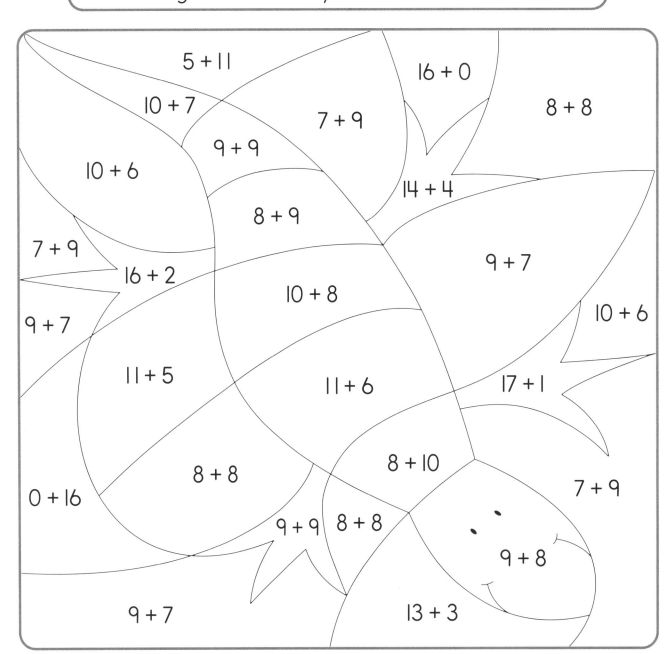

5 + 11

16 + 0

10 + 7

7 + 9

8 + 8

9 + 9

10 + 6

14 + 4

8 + 9

7 + 9

9 + 7

16 + 2

10 + 8

9 + 7

10 + 6

11 + 5

11 + 6

17 + 1

8 + 8

8 + 10

0 + 16

7 + 9

9 + 9   8 + 8

9 + 8

9 + 7   13 + 3

Addition Pyramids

Write the missing numbers to complete each pyramid. An example has been done for you.

Example:

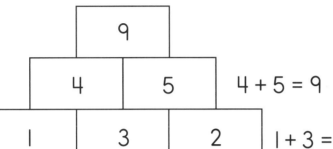

$4 + 5 = 9$

$1 + 3 = 4 \qquad 3 + 2 = 5$

1.

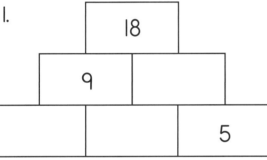

2.

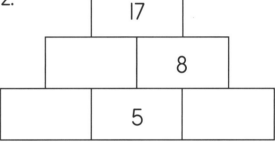

3.

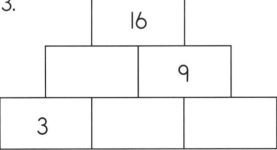

4.

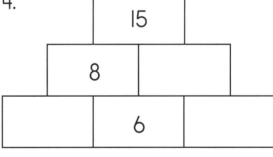

5.

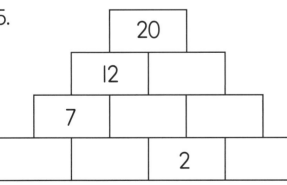

6.

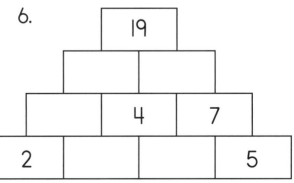

Fish Tank Facts

Color the pairs of fish in each tank with numbers that add up to the sum shown. Use a different color for each pair.

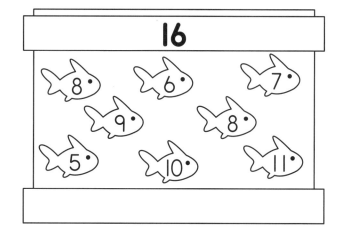

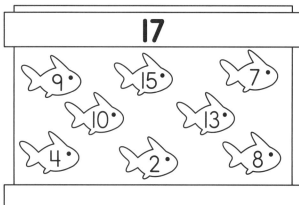

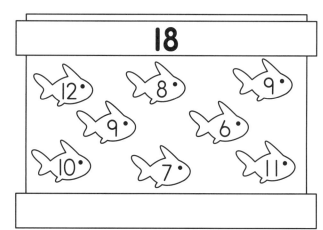

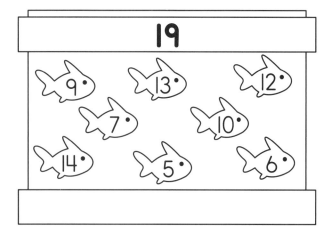

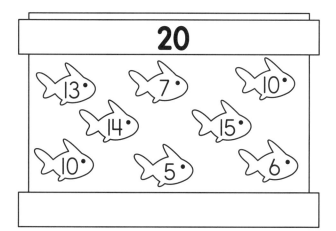

Name_____ Date_____

Round and Round

Draw lines from each sum to its facts.

14
8 + 6
7 + 9
2 + 12
11 + 3
10 + 4
9 + 6

15
6 + 9
4 + 11
0 + 14
9 + 3
10 + 5
7 + 8

16
6 + 11
8 + 8
11 + 4
5 + 7
10 + 6
2 + 14

17
12 + 6
5 + 12
4 + 13
6 + 4
8 + 9
7 + 10

13
12 + 0
10 + 3
1 + 11
9 + 4
8 + 5
6 + 7

18
17 + 1
2 + 10
16 + 4
6 + 9
7 + 11
8 + 10

19
12 + 9
10 + 9
6 + 15
2 + 17
3 + 16
11 + 8

12
10 + 2
4 + 6
7 + 5
6 + 3
8 + 2
6 + 6

A Sticky Riddle

Solve each problem. To solve the riddle, match the sums to the numbers and write the letters on the lines.

O 9 + 8 =

I 8 + 7 =

U 5 + 6 =

T 16 + 0 =

N 8 + 10 =

S 8 + 4 =

M 7 + 6 =

C 7 + 7 =

K 16 + 3 =

Y 17 + 3 =

What did the chewing gum say to the shoe?

"   ,

Answer: ___ ___   ___ ___ ___ ___ ___
            15 13   12 16 11 14 19

___ ___   ___ ___ ___!"
17 18   20 17 11

Name_____ Date_____

Purr-fect Pairs

Color each pair of numbers that add up to a sum in the bank. Color the pairs in order of sums 0–20. Pairs can be found across and down.

Ø	1	2	3	4	5	6	7	8	9	10
11	12	13	14	15	16	17	18	19	20	

0	0	10	8	3	6	5	4	2	1	7
2	1	0	1	9	2	2	3	6	1	10
1	5	9	1	2	1	9	2	2	5	8
3	4	5	8	3	7	1	1	5	4	9
6	5	9	3	1	7	2	8	10	3	4
4	6	8	7	8	6	9	4	6	1	7
4	0	8	5	6	8	2	6	9	4	6
8	3	8	9	8	2	0	6	2	6	3
0	4	0	1	9	7	2	3	8	5	5
1	10	9	10	9	1	10	1	3	10	0
9	10	1	6	0	7	2	4	2	8	7

Name_____ Date_____

Wild Addition

Solve each problem. Connect the dots in order from smallest sum to greatest sum.

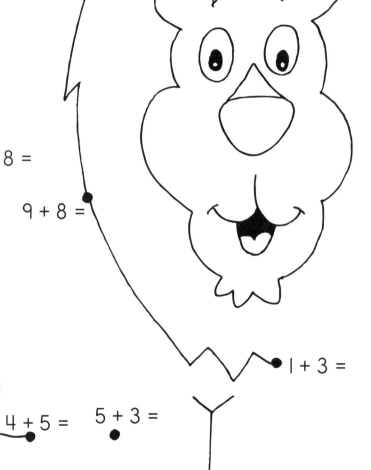

Start

1 + 0 =

1 + 1 =

8 + 7 =

7 + 7 =

1 + 2 =

8 + 8 =

6 + 7 =   9 + 8 =

1 + 3 =

4 + 5 =   5 + 3 =

5 + 5 =

1 + 4 =

6 + 6 =   7 + 4 =   4 + 3 =   3 + 3 =

CD-104577 • © Carson-Dellosa

Ring Toss

Find and draw rings around the pairs of numbers that add up to 20. Pairs can be found across, down, and diagonally. An example has been done for you.

4	2	20	16	7	16	19
18	17	6	0	14	1	4
15	5	5	12	8	13	9
12	2	18	3	15	11	4
13	20	6	16	7	10	10
1	7	5	8	4	17	19
9	14	6	18	0	11	3

Puzzling Problems

Cut out the puzzle pieces. Find the pieces with correct sums. Set aside the pieces with incorrect sums. On a separate sheet of paper, glue together the pieces with correct sums to form a picture.

$6 + 7 = 13$

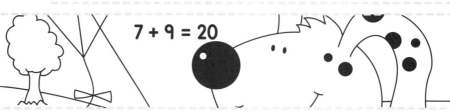

$7 + 9 = 20$

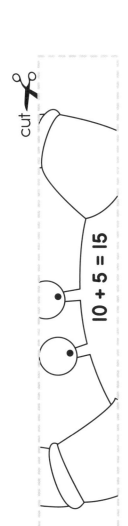

cut

$10 + 5 = 15$

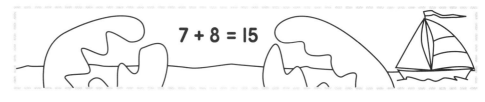

$7 + 8 = 15$

$9 + 9 = 18$

$8 + 8 = 16$

$5 + 9 = 14$

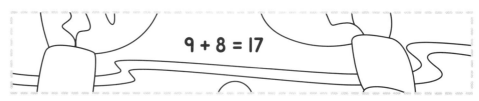

$9 + 8 = 17$

"Karate Belt" Bracelet Patterns

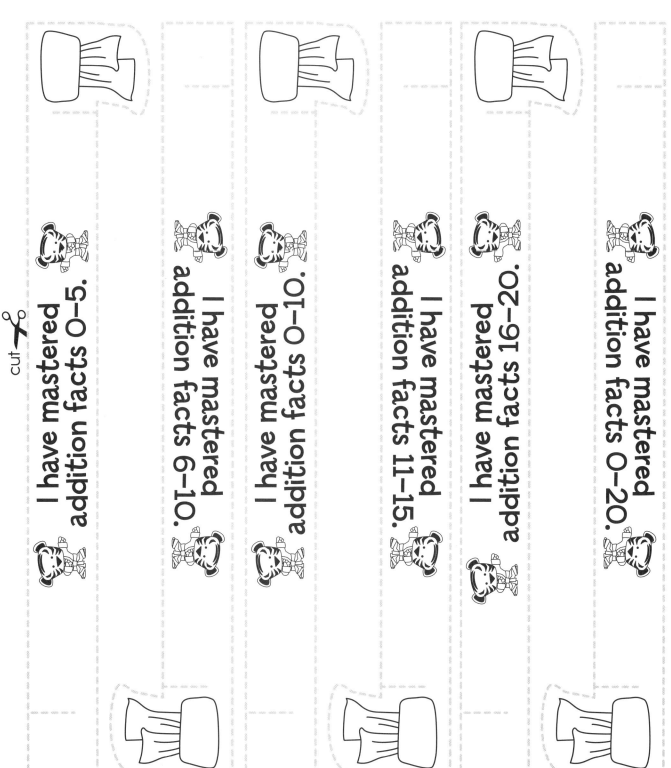

cut

I have mastered addition facts 0–5.

I have mastered addition facts 6–10.

I have mastered addition facts 0–10.

I have mastered addition facts 11–15.

I have mastered addition facts 16–20.

I have mastered addition facts 0–20.

congratulations!

_____

is a master of addition facts within 20.

_____

Page 4
Four birds should be glued onto the tree. One bird should be glued onto the ground. 4 + 1 = 5

Page 5
Check students' pictures.

Page 6
1. one + two = three; 2. zero + three = three; 3. four + one = five; 4. three + zero = three; 5. two + one = three; 6. two + zero = two; 7. five + zero = five; 8. three + one = four; 9. two + three = five; 10. one + zero = one

Page 7
1. 3; 2. 4; 3. 5; 4. 5; 5. 4; 6. 4; 7. 4; 8. 5; 9. 2

Page 8

Page 9
Check students' pictures.

Page 10
Check students' pictures.

Page 11
Answer: GLOVES

Page 12
1. 1; 2. 2; 3. 4; 4. 3; 5. 5; 6. 4; 7. 4; 8. 1; 9. 2; 10. 2; 11. 4; 12. 5; 13. 3; 14. 5; 15. 4; 16. 5; 17. 3; 18. 5

Page 13
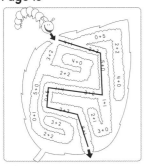

Page 14
1. 5 + 1 = 6; 2. 6 + 2 = 8; 3. 3 + 3 = 6; 4. 4 + 3 = 7; 5. 6 + 1 = 7; 6. 5 + 3 = 8; 7. 6 + 3 = 9; 8. 4 + 2 = 6; 9. 7 + 2 = 9; 10. 5 + 2 = 7; 11. 4 + 4 = 8; 12. 5 + 4 = 9; 13. 0 + 6 = 6; 14. 2 + 5 = 7; 15. 8 + 0 = 8

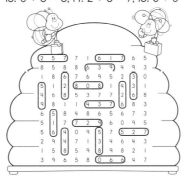

Page 15
Check students' pictures.

Page 16
6 = 6 + 0; 8 = 5 + 3 or 8 = 7 + 1; 10 = 1 + 9; 7 = 3 + 4; 9 = 5 + 4

Page 17

1.

1	0	1
1		2
2	1	3

2.

1	5	6
7		4
8	2	10

3.

6	0	6
2		4
8	2	10

4.

8	1	9
0		0
8	1	9

5.

6	0	6
1		3
7	2	9

6.

2	4	6
5		2
7	1	8

Page 18

$\frac{5}{+5}\ 10$	$\frac{4}{+3}\ 7$	$\frac{5}{+3}\ 8$	$\frac{2}{+6}\ 8$
$\frac{7}{+0}\ 7$	$\frac{3}{+7}\ 10$	$\frac{9}{+1}\ 10$	$\frac{0}{+8}\ 8$	$\frac{4}{+5}\ 9$
$\frac{5}{+1}\ 6$	$\frac{5}{+3}\ 8$	$\frac{6}{+4}\ 10$	$\frac{9}{+0}\ 9$	$\frac{2}{+7}\ 9$
$\frac{0}{+6}\ 6$	$\frac{7}{+3}\ 10$	$\frac{8}{+2}\ 10$	$\frac{3}{+5}\ 8$	$\frac{7}{+2}\ 9$
$\frac{1}{+8}\ 9$	$\frac{6}{+4}\ 10$	$\frac{6}{+2}\ 8$	$\frac{3}{+4}\ 7$
$\frac{9}{+0}\ 9$	$\frac{4}{+6}\ 10$	$\frac{8}{+2}\ 10$	$\frac{5}{+5}\ 10$

Page 19
6 = 4 + 2, 3 + 3, 5 + 1; 7 = 4 + 3, 2 + 5, 6 + 1; 8 = 1 + 7, 3 + 5, 2 + 6; 9 = 1 + 8, 5 + 4, 3 + 6; 10 = 7 + 3, 5 + 5, 6 + 4

Page 20

3 + 4	0 + 2	3 + 2		1 + 6	4 + 4	2 + 3
4 + 1	0 + 6	4 + 4		3 + 3	2 + 6	8 + 2
5 + 2	1 + 1			4 + 3	5 + 3	9 + 0

What is the sum? 6   What is the sum? 8

2 + 8	3 + 1			1 + 4	2 + 2	5 + 3
4 + 2	5 + 4	1 + 6		4 + 3		5 + 2
8 + 1	2 + 2	3 + 4		0 + 5	3 + 6	1 + 5

What is the sum? 9   What is the sum? 7

Page 21
Answer: "TENTICKLES"

Page 22
7 = 6 + 1, 3 + 4, and 5 + 2; 8 = 3 + 5, 4 + 4, and 2 + 6; 9 = 7 + 2 and 6 + 3

Page 23
1. 5 + 2 = 7; 0 + 9 = 9; 0 + 6 = 6; 4 + 4 = 8; 2. 1 + 5 = 6; 3 + 6 = 9; 2 + 8 = 10; 6 + 2 = 8; 3. 6 + 3 = 9; 5 + 1 = 6; 4 + 4 = 8; 5 + 1 = 6; 4. 2 + 5 = 7; 7 + 1 = 8; 2 + 7 = 9; 4 + 2 = 6; 5. 8 + 0 = 8; 3 + 6 = 9; 1 + 6 = 7; 0 + 7 = 7; 6. 1 + 8 = 9; 6 + 2 = 8; 0 + 6 = 6; 3 + 5 = 8; The car in lane 2 should be circled.

Page 24
1. 2 + 4 = 6; 2. 5 + 4 = 9; 3. 0 + 1 = 1; 4. 4 + 3 = 7; 5. 4 + 6 = 10; 6. 1 + 3 = 4; 7. 1 + 4 = 5; 8. 2 + 6 = 8; 9. 1 + 5 = 6; 10. 3 + 6 = 9; 11. 4 + 4 = 8; 12. 7 + 3 = 10; 13. 5 + 5 = 10; 14. 2 + 5 = 7; 15. 3 + 2 = 5

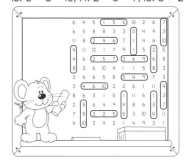

Page 25

Check students' coloring. The sum of each fact is 8.

Page 26

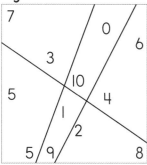

Page 27

Answer: A GOLDFISH

Page 28

1. 6 + 4 = 10; 2. 5 + 1 = 6; 3. 6 + 3 = 9;
4. 3 + 4 = 7; 5. 7 + 2 = 9; 6. 3 + 7 = 10;
7. 5 + 5 = 10; 8. 6 + 3 = 9; 9. 9 + 1 = 10;
10. 4 + 5 = 9; 11. 8 + 2 = 10; 12. 9 + 0 = 9

Page 29

7	9	14	1	3	0	4
8	2	9	8	7	13	11
0	3	13	2	9	6	1
15	8	4	8	7	5	3
11	3	10	7	15	1	4
4	12	5	14	4	8	11
2	9	6	8	3	15	0

Page 30

1. 6 + 9 = 15; 2. 8 + 3 = 11; 3. 7 + 8 = 15;
4. 5 + 8 = 13; 5. 4 + 8 = 12; 6. 4 + 9 = 13;
7. 9 + 3 = 12; 8. 2 + 9 = 11; 9. 5 + 9 = 14;
10. 6 + 8 = 14; 11. 9 + 2 = 11; 12. 7 + 7 = 14;
13. 6 + 6 = 12; 14. 10 + 3 = 13; 15. 9 + 6 = 15

Page 31

1. 11; 2. 13; 3. 12; 4. 12; 5. 15; 6. 14; 7. 15; 8. 15

Page 32

Answer: "THREE BLIND MICE"

Page 33

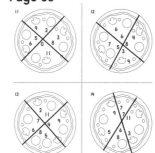

Page 34

Page 35

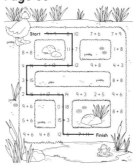

Page 36

Check students' pictures.

Page 37

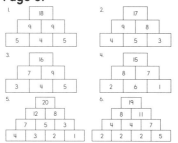

Page 38

16 = 8 + 8, 10 + 6, 5 + 11, and 9 + 7;
17 = 9 + 8, 10 + 7, 15 + 2, and 13 + 4;
18 = 9 + 9, 10 + 8, 7 + 11, and 12 + 6;
19 = 9 + 10, 6 + 13, 5 + 14, and 12 + 7;
20 = 10 + 10, 14 + 6, 5 + 15, and 13 + 7

Page 39

14 = 8 + 6, 10 + 4, 11 + 3, and 2 + 12;
17 = 4 + 13, 5 + 12, 7 + 10, and 8 + 9;

19 = 10 + 9, 11 + 8, 3 + 16, and 2 + 17;
16 = 8 + 8, 2 + 14, 10 + 6, and 9 + 7;
18 = 17 + 1, 9 + 9, 8 + 10, and 7 + 11;
15 = 6 + 9, 4 + 11, 10 + 5, and 7 + 8;
13 = 10 + 3, 6 + 7, 8 + 5, and 9 + 4;
12 = 10 + 2, 3 + 9, 6 + 6, and 7 + 5

Page 40

Answer: "I'M STUCK ON YOU!"

Page 41

Page 42

Check students' dot-to-dot pictures.

Page 43

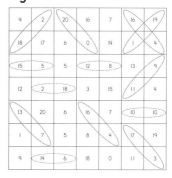

Page 44

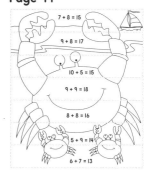